The faith to
FORGIVE

A New Path to Forgiveness
as a Journey of Faith

An imprint of Holy Impact Movement
311 Trenton Court, Murfreesboro, TN 37130

Copyright ©2018 by James McCarroll
All rights reserved.
ISBN - 978-1-7324070-3-9
Library of Congress Control Number - 2018914127

All Scripture quotations, unless otherwise indicated are taken from the Holy Bible, New Revised Standard Version Bible, copyright © 1989 National Council of the Churches of Christ in the United States of America. Used by permission. All rights reserved worldwide.

Thank you Alicia Smith for editing this work. Also, thank you Elma McKnight and Barbara Tuckson for serving as proofreaders for this work. Finally, thank you Dr. Brittany Lee for your counsel and for providing the Foreword for this project.

Cover Design: Davy Mac Promotional

Interior Design: James McCarroll
Printed in the United States of America

Published by Holy Impact Publishing, LLC
holyimpactmovement.org

To the One who specializes in
fully restoring broken hearts.

Table of Contents

Before you begin this journey...	1
The Mercy Ethic	7
Forgiveness is a Matter of Faith	18
The Faith to Face the Hurt	30
The Faith to Let it Go	48
The Faith to Reclaim a Healthy Life	66
A Closing Word...	79
Endnotes	80

FOREWORD
By Dr. Brittany Lee

This book has the potential to be life-changing. What you hold in your hand is no ordinary, run-of-the-mill book about forgiveness. The concept of forgiveness and the importance of this virtue, as mandated to us by the LORD, is not a foreign concept to many who have picked up this book. We have been taught to forgive since the "dawn of day" and have learned age old adages including, "Forgive and Forget" and "Let bygones be bygones" from our parents, teachers, and authority figures in our developmental years. Forgiveness was illustrated to us first-hand in the book of Genesis, as we read of the reconciliation between Joseph and his brothers. And of utmost significance to Christians, is the glorious redemptive story of Jesus Christ, who the Father sent to conquer evil and forgive us of our sins. Yes, we are aware of the definition of forgiveness, we can cite stories about the topic, and we can even acknowledge the necessity of it in our daily lives. So then why do we, as a people, continue to struggle with forgiving? It is my belief that this book not only succeeds in answering this question, but aids the reader in gaining a better understanding in the journey that is forgiveness. This book seeks to go beyond educating you about forgiveness, and strives to cultivate an internal experience that will undoubtedly change your life.

As a Licensed Clinical Psychologist, I have had my fair share of engaging in therapeutic work centered around forgiveness. My clinical experiences have allowed me to serve veterans, individuals in the community, adults with developmental disabilities, and even college students. I have worked with multiculturally diverse populations who differ in terms of race/ethnicity, age, gender, gender identity, sexual orientation, socioeconomic status, religion, and disability status. What has constantly come up in all of my work with such diverse individuals is their personal struggle with forgiveness. Whether the individual's struggle has related to forgiveness of a parental figure or caregiver, a spouse or partner, a perpetrator, and even of self, it continues to permeate the therapeutic space.

After learning of Reverend James McCarroll's personal journey to and through forgiveness and his passion about leading others through their own journey, I was excited for the opportunity to be a part of this project. In reading the manuscript, not only was I pulled towards the authenticity of the writing but the practicality of the message. What I found in reading this book was not just tips and tricks for the reader to forgive, but permission to experience the pain and anger that result from an infraction. Readers are provided with the understanding of the impact of their unforgiveness and its effect on their relationships with others. They are informed that it is okay to set boundaries and that there is wisdom in doing so. Readers are given the words to pray when they continue to be reminded of the painful experience and find themselves angry all over again. Most importantly, readers are enlightened to the understanding that forgiveness is a journey and not a one-time deal. It is something that one will likely come back to time and time again. And that is okay.

Are there areas in your life where you see the need for healing? How have you suffered as a result of your unforgiveness? What opportunities have been missed? What relationships have been destroyed? James McCarroll helps you to find the answer to these questions and more. As you journey through this book, you will begin your own voyage of discovery which I believe will ultimately end in positive growth, increased faith, and magnanimous wisdom.

Before you begin this journey...

Forgiveness is defined by Merriam Webster as, "ceasing to feel resentment against (an offender); to pardon." I didn't learn this thing called, "forgiveness" in the Sunday school classroom, a softened church pew, or in some Christian tutorial session. The place where I learned forgiveness was much different and not as carefully wrapped. I learned it in the shadows of some of the most hurtful experiences my heart has ever felt. It was discovered in a moment where my heart was caught in the middle of a tug-of-war between grace and vengeance. Like many of you that will read this book, the lesson on real forgiveness took place in a much more challenging space where the decision to forgive was not one at which there was an easy arrival.

I've learned over the years, that we really don't learn forgiveness in comfortable, convenient and neatly designed Christian education spaces. That's where we learn of forgiveness. We learn forgiveness when our hearts are still beating at high rates every time the memory pops up in our minds of what was done to us. It's learned in spaces where our confidence has been shattered and we feel as though our trust has been compromised. We learn forgiveness in spaces that are wrapped in fear and cloaked in trauma. We learn forgiveness in spaces where our commentary of the hurtful moment can't start or conclude without repeating the phrases "I don't believe they did that to me "or "How could I let that happen?" Forgiveness is learned in the parking lots of our destinies - those places where we've placed our love and our belief in those around us in neutral for fear that if we move forward we will face another episode of hurt.

So if you're in that place at this moment it's okay. This book is not about learning the definition of forgiveness. It's about walking you through the space where you learn practical forgiveness. You may be in the corridor of the pain facing every potentially joyful moment with hesitation because you have deafened your ears and your mind to possibility due to the echoes of your hurts in yesterdays passed. You may be wondering if forgiveness is worth it because you think you'll set yourself up for failure or a rehearsal of disappointment.

That is why the title of this book is "The Faith to Forgive". Forgiveness requires more than head knowledge. It requires the ability to find confidence in the space where you have to begin again, trust again, believe again, and hope again.

Before you turn the next page and begin this

book, I want you to ask yourself one question, "Am I ready to let go of my yesterdays' hurt so that I can embrace tomorrow's hope?" Because if you're not, close the book, place it back on the shelf, and wait until such a time as you are ready to forgive. However, if you are ready to proceed into the rest of your life of freedom, love, trust, and restored relationships, then let's begin. But if you begin, make a promise to yourself that you will not stop until you've finished the journey.

Now let's go into the next chapter of your life.

A Look Within...

1. Although we know that simply knowing the definition of forgiveness does not serve to help you to actually forgive, what is your definition of forgiveness? Reflect on what has shaped your understanding of forgiveness and write the core principles of forgiveness that you have adopted.

2. Have you ever thought to yourself, "Is forgiveness worth it?" Maybe you believed that you were better off forgetting this hurt ever occurred. What makes forgiveness worth it?

3. What thoughts and feelings arise for you as you contemplate beginning this journey of forgiveness (fear, excitement, dread, joy, etc.)? Take a moment to describe what you are feeling internally.

The Mercy Ethic

"Forgiveness is the fragrance that the violet sheds on the heel that has crushed it."

–Mark Twain

The motive behind the wrestling that many people have with forgiveness is often misunderstood. It is not uncommon to think that our reason for not forgiving is based upon some superficial emotional or social rationale that perceives the withholding of an offense as a healthy defensive tactic for the greater good of personal health and relationship safety. We use reasons like not being hurt again, "teaching the person a lesson" or even making "wise" decisions as our underlying motive for keeping the offense present in our hearts and minds. Though these may have validity at some levels, they are not the true "center" of our inability and/or unwillingness to forgive. The real reason that we won't forgive can be summed up in two words, our ethics.

According to Merriam Webster, ethics are defined as "a set of moral principles; a theory or system of moral values." In essence, ethics are the guiding principles that each of us uses to determine whether things are good or bad. They are the lens through which we measure every action, impulse and thought and conclude whether it is the right or wrong thing to do. Each major decision that we make or don't make and the subsequent choices that precede and succeed those major decisions are reflections of our ethical framework. Ultimately, when it comes to forgiveness, how and when we forgive is a reflection of our ethical lens.

For instance, a person may assume that forgiveness should be granted for a minor offense like a person accidentally stepping on his or her shoe, but it shouldn't be granted if that same person breaks his or her heart. Such a decision is based upon a person's moral values and how they understand what is considered to be the "right" response.

Each area of our lives has an ethic attached to it. There is a spending/saving ethic attached to your finances, a work/rest ethic attached to your work routine, a parenting ethic attached to how you raise your children and the list goes on and on. When it comes to forgiveness, the main ethical concern is who should be shown compassion and, in turn, receive pardon from the offense. This system of expressing or not expressing compassion is what I term the "mercy ethic." It is the basis for determining which person(s) in our lives should be the recipients of compassion and mercy in the moment of offense.

It is our mercy ethic that determines when and how we forgive. As identified by Nancy Demoss in her book *Choosing Forgiveness*, it determines when we operate as what she calls "debt collectors" or "debt releasers." This language is based on Demoss' consideration of the parable of the unforgiving servant found in Matthew 18:22-34. In this parable, a man that has been forgiven of a significantly large debt refuses to forgive the person that owes him a very minimal amount. Demoss' language points to the fact that people that choose not to forgive become "debt collectors" – meaning that they make it a point to keep a record of all that has been done offensively towards them and make it a priority to hold others emotionally or socially hostage until the debt has been "paid in full." Conversely, those that make it a point to forgive choose to be "debt releasers" – meaning that they refuse to exact vengeance or demand payment of offenses. Instead, they release the debt and allow the person to experience the compassion of their hearts. The difference between these mercy ethics, according to the parable, is one's remembrance of the compassion which was granted to them.

In counseling, I have found that people that hold on to the hurtful actions of others have usually granted themselves permission to have voluntary amnesia about their own need for compassion. The mercy ethic is a direct reflection of our personal awareness and acknowledgement of the mercy that we have received that we really did not deserve. Whether that mercy is coming from God or other people, it serves to remind us of how much our current existence is the result of someone else's benevolence and how possible it is that the roles could be reversed at any moment.

Rodney Hogue, in his book *Forgiveness*, states, "When we receive [God's] love for us, we become infused with a love from above that is far beyond what this world offers. We become empowered to love with God's love. It is a love that does not require love in return. It is a love that overshadows the sins of others and becomes the dominant ruling force in our life."[1] When we notice the mercy that we have received, we become more willing to extend that mercy to others. However, when we choose not to remember the mercy that we have received, then we have a greater tendency to punish others for the acts that they have committed against us.

Also in this parable, there is another element of the mercy ethic that is uncovered. When the forgiven man chooses not to forgive the debt of his fellow servant, the King calls that man back into His presence. Once there, the man is informed that because of his unwillingness to show mercy after he was granted mercy, the debt that was previously forgiven is going to be reinstated. He becomes subjected to what John Bevere calls "You don't give – you don't get." [2] This is to remind us that the mercy that we show has an impact on the mercy that we will receive in the future (from both God and others – see Matthew 5:7; Galatians 5:15). As stated by St. Francis of Assissi, "It is in pardoning that we are pardoned."[3]

Which label best describes you: debt collector or debt releaser? There is probably a little of both in you. The fact that you are reading this book is an indication that there are most likely one or more areas of your life in which you are having a hard time moving from debt collector to debt releaser. If so, that's perfectly fine. It is an indication that this book is for you. Rest assured that it is not uncommon, nor is it incurable. If your heart is open to what will be introduced in the pages to come, not only will it find healing, it will experience a shift in mercy.

A Prayer to Become a "Debt Releaser"

Heavenly Father, I realize that there are areas in which I have difficulty releasing the offenses of others. I confess this struggle to You and ask for grace to help me open my heart to give the same mercy towards others that I receive from you. I grant you permission to search my heart and remove any spiritual, emotional or mental hindrances that would prevent me from loving in a way that reflects your heart. Deposit your love into my heart so that I can deposit that same love into the lives of others. Thank you for hearing my prayer. In Jesus' name, I ask this. AMEN.

A Look Within...

1.   How is your mercy ethic depicted (size of the offense, the person who offends, how you feel, etc.)?

2.   Can you recognize moments in your life in which you were granted forgiveness and then subsequently withheld forgiveness from another person? Did you realize it quickly? How can being mindful of the grace and compassion of God help you to grant mercy in the same manner to others?

3.   Can you identify any hindrances that get in the way of your willingness to forgive (spiritual, emotional, mental, behavioral)?

Forgiveness is a Matter of Faith

"As an alternative to being debt collectors, the pathway of resentment and retaliation – God calls us to the pure, powerful choice of forgiveness – and to pursue, wherever possible, the pathway of restoration and reconciliation."

– Nancy Demoss, Choosing Forgiveness

In Luke chapter 17, Jesus gives one of the most outlined and methodical models for forgiveness in the entire bible. He describes how we should respond after we have been offended by others. After this discussion, Jesus makes a statement that would shake the foundation of anyone that is "reasonably" compassionate. He says, "if a person sins against you seven times in a day and seven times returns to you saying, 'I repent,' you shall forgive him." Can't you hear the inner voice of the disciples saying, "Now Jesus, it's one thing to forgive, but this is taking it way too far!" They – like many of us – most likely wrestled with the logic and "fairness" of such a commandment. But what is most intriguing is how they responded to this statement. They respond by saying to the Lord, "Increase our faith." Doesn't it seem rather strange that they didn't ask the Lord to increase their love or patience? Why not ask for more wisdom or mercy? It is this response that prompted me to write this book.

Most conversations that we have concerning why we don't forgive are centered around our questioning of whether we have enough love or patience for others. This usually becomes the conversation because we are thinking about our direct relationship and considering what is spiritually misaligned or displaced within us that would cause us to withhold the hurt and settle for a breach in the relationship. Such things like love, patience, understanding and wisdom are addressed because we are trying to figure out what needs to be fixed within our hearts that will yield a space of forgiveness.

The disciples skip that entire conversation. The remedy for them is not an emotional or social adjustment. It is a spiritual one. They ask for increased faith. In order to understand why they would – and we should – request a faith upgrade, we need to review the concept of faith. Simply put, faith can be defined as confidence in the plan, promise and/or power of God that is forthcoming despite the present tangible or intangible facts (Hebrews 11:1). It is an assurance that God can produce an outcome that defies the logically expected conclusion of the present circumstances.

Faith is a spiritual reality that comes from a change in perception. According to Romans 10:17, it is the product of hearing the Word of God. In other words, faith isn't produced from willpower or human intellect. It comes from a holy encounter in which God gives you a vision for how He desires our lives to look after He has moved supernaturally on our behalf. In essence, faith shows you a picture of your life that you can only produce with God. So when the disciples ask for their faith to be increased, they are asking the Lord to increase their confidence to see and believe that the outcome of such forgiveness could be reached.

For many of us, that is the real issue. Although there are some love concerns, it's not the primary concern. Perhaps we have a mercy shortage, but that isn't the major deficiency. The real challenge that we face is being able to see ourselves and our relationships the way that God apparently sees them. We wrestle with seeing ourselves as being able to let multiple offenses go. We wonder if a relationship could suffer that many offenses and still be restored to a healthy state of being. Therefore, I think that it is only fitting that we take the space to discover the "type of faith" that is needed if our relationships are ever going to be restored and reconnected so that they can live beyond the hurt and pain that they will inevitably face.

Faith as a mustard seed

Just as interesting as the disciples' response to Jesus is Jesus' next statement. He says to them, "If you have faith as a mustard seed, you can say to this mulberry tree, 'Be pulled up by the roots and be planted in the sea,' and it would obey you." Jesus not only affirms their request, but qualifies it. He reminds them that it is not the quantity of faith, but the type of faith that makes the difference. We all know people that have great faith, but are still unable to forgive others. Forgiveness takes a special kind of faith, "faith as a mustard seed."

Why would Jesus use the metaphor of a mustard seed? Those of us who were reared in church environments automatically relate this statement to the size of a mustard seed. We think about the fact that a mustard seed is small and assume that Jesus is telling us that as long as we have a little faith we can do great things. This is based upon the conversation that Jesus has about the size of a mustard seed in Matthew 13:31-32 in the parable comparing the mustard seed to the Kingdom of heaven. However, the nature of the aforementioned verse is not comparable to the nature of this verse on forgiveness. Furthermore, we see Jesus identifying "little faith" as a negative attribute to have as a Christian (Matthew 16:8). The more comparable verse is found in Matthew 17:20. In this passage on faith, it is pertaining to casting the demon out of a boy who had suffered with seizures. The reference to faith as a mustard seed was used to denote faith that could speak to a mountain and witness it move at one's command.

In each of these passages, the faith of a mustard seed is directly relating to the uprooting or movement of something that was difficult to dislodge and/or displace. In Luke, it refers to the releasing of an offense. In Matthew, it refers to the removal of a demon. The common pattern points to "mustard seed" faith as a spiritual tool that has the ability to move that which is seemingly immoveable. Such a description doesn't seem to be commensurate with the size of a mustard seed, but it is much more fitting if we look at a mustard seed medicinally. In the day and times of our text, mustard seeds were used as an expectorant. According to Rosalee De La Forét in her book, *Alchemy of Herbs*, "Using a mustard seed poultice directly over the lungs has been a long-lived tradition to help people with congested lungs and bronchitis. The spicy stimulating properties of the mustard seeds increase and thin mucus secretions, making it easier for the body to expel them from the lungs."[4] Similar to medicine like Mucinex™, it was used to dislodge mucus in the lungs and bronchial tubes. Thus, the reference to "mustard seed" faith makes sense. It is faith that can uproot things that "need to be spiritually dislodged" and don't come out naturally.

This is why it is so important with forgiveness. Faith as a "mustard seed" is faith that enables us to see and believe God's planned outcome in such a way that we begin to uproot those elements that work against it. We begin to envision the restored relationship and releasing of offenses with a new level of confidence and we respond accordingly. Not only does our perception change, but the way we speak changes as well.

In both passages, Jesus immediately follows the statement concerning "mustard seed" faith with the language that is produced from it. He teaches us that when this type of faith fills our hearts, we will speak to our offenses with confidence instead of compliance. As Jesus states in Luke, we will speak to the tree of offense until it becomes uprooted. When you get "mustard seed" faith, your language will no longer be limited to simply describing what's going on. It will seek to align your heart with God's planned reality for its health and wholeness.

Before you can forgive, you must first assess your faith. Can you see yourself as loving enough to let the hurt go? Can you see the possibility of a restored and healthy relationship? If you can't then you may want to take a moment and ask the Lord to "increase your faith" using this prayer for increased faith.

A Prayer for Increased Faith

Heavenly Father, I know that you are calling me to forgive. However, I have a hard time seeing beyond my disappointment and hurt. Grant my heart the grace for "mustard seed" faith that will allow me to see the possibility that lies in You. Then, grant me the grace that will give me the courage to speak in a way that will uproot and evict the root of bitterness from my heart. Thank you for being a God that makes forgiveness possible. In Jesus' name I ask this. AMEN

A Look Within...

1. How does seeing forgiveness as a matter of faith instead of love change your thinking about it?

2. Do you speak to your offenses with confidence or compliance? Is your language attempting to align your heart with God's hope or affirm your heart in the acceptance of past hurt? How does the perspective of your faith need to change?

3. Take an assessment of your type of faith - as it pertains to forgiveness. What are some things you have discovered about the nature of your faith?

III

The Faith to Face the Hurt

We all need healing and reconciliation in our lives. It takes willingness and work, but the rewards are huge. And on the other side of the process is freedom, for you and for others, as well as joy in walking in the path God has laid before us.

– Adam Hamilton, Forgiveness

I'm stronger than this.

It shouldn't hurt like this.

There is no way that I will let them get to me.

I'm okay. I just got caught off-guard.

It doesn't hurt. I'm just disappointed.

These are some of the lies that we tell ourselves after our hearts have been broken. These are the masks that we choose to wear so that we don't appear weak, vulnerable or scared. As Brené Brown, in her book *Daring Greatly* suggests, "...when we dare greatly we will err and we will come up short again and again. There will be failures and mistakes and criticism. If we want to be able to move through the difficult disappointments, the hurt feelings, and the heartbreaks that are inevitable in a fully lived life, we can't equate defeat with being unworthy to love, belonging and joy. If we do, we'll never show up and try again."[5]

As Jesus reminds us in Luke 17:1, at some point in this life, each of us will have an encounter that offends us. Every person will have something happen that causes an emotional wound. Whether it comes at the hand of a dear friend, an "enemy," a babysitter-turned-child-abuser, an adulterous spouse, the other thousands of people that we know that can potentially offend us and/or God Himself, hurt, disappointment and/or disaster will eventually find our address and pay a visit to our lives. Inevitably, all of us will get hurt.

Though all of us will eventually experience hurt, it will not be the same for everyone and it will not be the same every time. Some hurt will be small disappointments (like forgetting to put cheese on a hamburger or leaving a door unlocked). Other hurts have a much greater emotional impact (like being sexually assaulted or losing a family member in a automobile accident involving a drunk driver). Whether they are small or large, each carries an emotional impact on our lives.

I believe that Jesus included this truth in Luke because we attempt to exclude it from our recollections and recounts of the event. We remember the details, anger and the resulting distrust, but we don't really take the time to allow ourselves to acknowledge how the action impacted us at a heart level. There must be space made for us to accept the REAL hurt that this event or series of events has introduced into our lives.

Accept the Hurt

There are numerous reasons that we choose to overlook or minimize the hurt that we feel. For some of us, it is a sign of weakness. For others, it exposes our "buttons" and opens us up to future offenses. But regardless of the reason(s), we often try to avert the truth that we are experiencing a very real pain. This is the first step to forgiveness. Where there is no hurt, there can be no healing. Nancy Demoss points out that "...unacknowledged and unaddressed, its poison will affect and infect you and others beyond anything you ever imagined possible."[6] Most of us have been hurt by one of the following encounters:

Disappointment
Rejection
Abandonment
Ridicule
Humiliation
Betrayal

Deception
Abuse

Which one(s) of these words best describe the offense that has hurt you the most deeply?

As we prepare our hearts to re-forge the hope of a new beginning, we must start by asking ourselves, "How did this make me feel in my heart?" Lay aside the ego, machismo, pride, arrogance and "Superman" or "Superwoman" complex. Realize that you are still human and possess feelings that can be injured. Then, give yourself permission to hurt. Feel the sting and trauma at whatever level it REALLY exists.

It is in the experience and acceptance of this hurt that we truly face the moment. Don't attempt to minimize it or make light of it. Feel the sting and stench of the disappointment of the moment and the bruising of your soul. Acknowledge that - in the moment - it left an impression on you in a way that left you in a wounded state. Give yourself permission to see the hurt for what it is and how it is impacting your life.

Living with "hurt echoes"

The sad but true reality is that the moment of hurt is over. However, we experience its affects because we make it a point to replay it in our minds. We live and breathe in the echoes of its reality. The threat is long past, but the footprints of its presence in our lives are still kept fresh by our memories. As Demoss says, "The root of bitterness will infest every inch of ground in your life if you let it."[7] If we are not careful, we will set up a tent and find permanent dwelling in the shadows of an experience that has passed its expiration date for inhabiting our hearts.

As Thich Naht Hanh, in his book *Fear*, states: "Some of us have depression and continue to suffer even if in the present situation everything looks all right. This is because we have a tendency to dwell in the past. We feel more comfortable making our home there, even if it holds a lot of suffering. That home is deep down in our subconscious, where the films are always projected. Every night you go back and watch those films and suffer. And the future you constantly worry about is nothing other than a projection of fear and desire from the past."[8]

These echoes are more than just emotional recounting, the psychological experience is as real as when it happened. Revisiting the memory still causes our hearts to race and our blood pressure to elevate. Any small trigger can immediately place us back in the moment and all that was included therein. It still hurts even after the offense has come and gone. In those moments we shift from experiencing what psychologists call "natural emotions" and begin developing "manufactured emotions."

In their book, *Cognitive Processing Therapy for PTSD*, Resick, Monson, and Chard state:

"Humans are hard-wired to have natural emotions in response to threat, loss, something disgusting, or even something pleasant… However, once the danger is over, a person should return to a steady state… Emotions of the other kind are generated by the client's thoughts following the event. These emotions produced by thoughts are what we call 'manufactured emotions…'"[9]

This hurt and the subsequent "manufactured emotions" that have been birthed from it have been tinting the lens though which you see your story. Reacquaint yourself with how much permission you have given it to exist in spaces that were totally detached from and unrelated to the space in which it was introduced. How many people have you accused as guilty though their actions were clearly innocent? Even worse, how have you infected your own life by continuing to poison your self-perception with the recounting of the hurt? There are countless people who have pursued life's greatest blessings (relationships, jobs, family, etc.) with a warped understanding of themselves and the world around them because they live allowing their vision to be influenced by their deepest hurt. Robert Hogue speaks about this in his book, *Forgiveness*, when he states:

"Sometimes a person's life can be shaped by his or her offenders. You can turn into a person that isn't who you really are based on how others have related to you. In your hurts and wounds, you could develop unwanted behavioral patterns in how you relate to others. How you relate to people, how you react, how close you get to others are directly affected by how others have hurt you." [10]

Much of the personal dysfunction pertaining to our identity and other negative factors originate with some deeper area of offense. They are merely attempts to run as far away as we can get from the person (or people like him/her) or situation (or similar situations) as possible. As Matthew Kelly states in his book, Resisting Happiness, "The path of least resistance effortlessly creates negative rituals, routines and rhythms."[11] We equate relocation with healing – when they are not the same.

Beware of the "Collateral Damage"

It would be a little better if the hurt remained localized and didn't spread beyond the moment. However, our distress tends to bleed into the other areas and relationships in our lives. When we hurt, we tend to make other people feel the effects of it. They are forced to deal with the aftershocks that come from our disappointment. Relationships, workplaces, customers, ministries, commitment, and a host of other things have to face environments that have been influenced by a hurt that they did not prompt.

As we accept the hurt, we must also embrace the truth of how much of our lives have been impacted by it. The affects influence more of our lives than we really think. Dr. Sidney Simon in his book, *Forgiveness*, speaks to how unforgiveness has been proven to have an effect on our lives at several different levels:

"What's more, collecting injustices, holding grudges, and walking around with unresolved and unexpressed anger boiling inside us takes its toll on our physical health and emotional well-being. It creates stress, elevates blood pressure, increases stomach acidity, contributing to such physical ailments as ulcers, colitis, and arthritis. Our grievances hang around our neck like invisible albatrosses, and we get backaches, chest pains, anxiety attacks, and migraine headaches. With our heart racing and adrenaline pumping, our head spinning and our ears ringing, holding a grudge just plain does not feel good."[12]

And neither does the emotional fallout that accompanies it. Nursing our wounds, we withdraw, have difficulty maintaining friendships, are generally intolerant, and are unable to look at events from other people's perspectives. We become suspicious and hypersensitive, more likely to be hurt again, always ready to start an argument, forgetful, subtly uncooperative. Our negativity and bitterness alienates everyone around us, and we are left alone, lonely, high up in our tower of righteous indignation with only our pain and fantasies of revenge for our company. This is not where we wanted to go, but it is always where holding a grudge takes us.

Also, we have to own our unhealthy behavior in other areas and realize that it is the collateral damage of a single hurtful event. As Demoss states, "When we fail to deal with our hurts

God's way, when we harbor resentment in our hearts, that bitterness—like an infection—will fester and work its way into our system, until ultimately we start viewing everything through the eyes of hurt—everything others do, everything that happens to us."[13] In many cases, the hurt causes a response that Dr. Sidney Simon calls "victimization." Dr. Simon states:

"Victimization describes what happened to you. A specific event or series of events…may have hurt you, terrified you, or took something that you needed away from you… Once we have been victimized, we never forget it. The sense of helplessness and hopelessness that we felt at that time is filed away in our subconscious mind. And as a result, we are likely to feel like a victim whenever we encounter situations that seem to be forced upon us or require us to do things that we do not want to do – even though these situations may bear little or no resemblance to the events that first elicited those feelings. When we encounter situations that we perceive as being beyond our control, the victim part of us takes over and we pay a visit to the victim stage....You may complain about the situation but do nothing to change it; not assert yourself; become wishy-washy, hypersensitive, or belligerent—lashing out at everyone and everything but the real source of your anger. "[14]

Knowing that we are in a space that has been shaped by hurt, there must be great intentionality taken to be cautious in how we view and respond to others. An understanding and healthy acceptance of the affect that our hurt has on our lives will lead to a healthy understanding of how we may be allowing it to warp our personal spaces and relationships. In order to minimize the collateral damage, we must revisit the boundaries of our pain and be careful not to allow them to have a toxic affect on the lives of those around us.

Forgiveness begins with having the faith to allow ourselves to be hurt. It is necessary that we allow the reality of our hurt to be permitted as part of our existence. But as we give ourselves permission to hurt, let us make sure that we aren't granting the pain permission to operate with unhealthy parameters. Our hurt was never intended to become infectious to the hearts and lives of others. Therefore, choose to hurt, but refuse to be hurtful.

A Prayer for the Courage to Face the Hurt

Heavenly Father, there have been some experiences that have taken place that brought deep and lasting hurt into my life. Unsuccessfully, I have tried to get around focusing on them. I need You to give me the courage and grace to face my hurt and the memories associated with them so that I can position myself to release them. Sustain my heart as I journey to those places of pain. Grant me the grace needed to experience the hurt, but also, move from the hurt to a place of healing. In Jesus' name, I ask this. AMEN

A Look Within...

1. What's under your "mask?" Identify the emotions surrounding the offense that comes to mind.

2. Have you given yourself permission to hurt or do you internalize it? What does it mean to acknowledge and accept your emotions? What does the process look like to you?

3. Think about your most hurtful offense. What emotions did you feel at the time? Since time has passed, have you also experienced anger/blame at yourself for "allowing this to happen" because you "should have known better?"

4. In what areas of your life (relationships, work, ministry, etc.) have suffered due to your struggle with not acknowledging and/or accepting your pain?

The Faith to Let it Go

The person who gains the most from forgiveness is the person who does the forgiving.

–R.T. Kendall, Total Forgiveness

In the 1960's, Jack Dempsey, an American professional boxer in the early 1900's, had a saying that was often used: "The best defense is a good offense." If we are going to see the benefits of healthy relationships, it will only be realized when we understand how to properly handle conflict. Considering the survival instinct that is inherently placed within each of us to highlight and avert danger, it is not unusual that we would become intentional about recounting, rehearsing and finding ways to not repeat those things that hurt us. As stated by Matthew Lieberman in his book, *Social: Why Our Brains are Wired to Connect*, "Psychologically, we are more sensitive to losses so we try to avoid what feels like a sure loss."[15] This concept is called, loss aversion. It suggests that when we approach a scenario similar to one in which we have a history of hurt, we are more prone to not embrace it. This response can be seen in many of our human relationships as well. We have a problem letting go of offenses because we feel that such a response is not a healthy defense to secure "safe" relationships. We have what author Jonathan Haidt calls a "negative affective lifestyle." As stated in his book, *The Happiness Hypothesis*, "...people who have a negative affective style...live in a world filled with many more threats and have less confidence that they can deal with them. They develop a coping style that relies more heavily on avoidance and other defensive mechanisms. They work harder to manage their pain than to fix their problems, so their problems often get worse."[16] However, the scriptures remind us over 20 times of the benefits (both short and long-term) of forgiveness. As Hogue states, "The only way to be free is to release the debt. In releasing the debt you are releasing your tie to the debtor, and the result is freedom."[17]

It is not uncommon to approach the space of forgiveness with some level of concern that you are positioning yourself to face numerous negative outcomes - from being hurt again to offering your life as a "punching bag" - to any person that comes along. It is necessary that you understand what forgiveness is not:

1. Forgiveness is not forgetting.
2. Forgiveness is not condoning.
3. Forgiveness is not absolution.
4. Forgiveness is not a form of self-sacrifice.
5. Forgiveness is not a clear-cut, one-time decision.[18]

In the same way that the negative perceptions work against our decision to forgive, we must also gain positive perceptions that will fuel our desire to forgive. In order to do this, we need to understand what forgiveness is:

1. Forgiveness is a by-product of an ongoing healing process.
2. Forgiveness is a sign of positive self-esteem.
3. Forgiveness is letting go of the intense emotions attached to incidents from our past.
4. Forgiveness is recognizing that we no longer need our grudges and resentments, our hatred and self-pity.
5. Forgiveness is no longer wanting to punish people who hurt us.
6. Forgiveness is accepting that nothing we do to punish them will heal us.
7. Forgiveness is freeing up and putting to better use the energy once consumed by holding grudges, harboring resentments, and nursing unhealed wounds.
8. Forgiveness is moving on.[19]

So how do you do it? What does forgiveness

include? There are several components to forgiveness that allow it to be truly effective.

It begins within

Forgiveness doesn't begin with you addressing or confronting another person about why or how they hurt you. It begins with you asking yourself, "Exactly what hurt me and how bad does it hurt?" The first question, "Exactly what hurt me?" will require you to sift through the flood of emotions to find the specific offense that triggered the hurt. It's not enough to just recall the scenario, there must be an identifying of the emotional trauma that led to you feeling offended. For instance, a person that was sexually assaulted would initially state that they are hurt because they were sexually assaulted. However, the more accurate identification of the offense would be that they felt and believed they were robbed of significance and their value and voice in that moment was violated. They may also feel as though they were unprotected and left exposed by those that loved them – including God. These are the types of emotionally-disturbing perceptions (or misperceptions) that are at the root of the offense and need to be forgiven. Hogue states, "If the root is spiritual in nature, then the only complete cure is to address the issue on a spiritual level. Otherwise, you have disease management instead of healing."[20]

Take a moment and write the area(s) of emotional offense on a sheet of paper. Make sure that they are easy to read so that you can revisit them later in the process.

The second question, "How bad does it hurt?" also needs to be addressed. Every offense prompts an emotional response. In many cases, the depth and intensity of the raw response is repressed because it would lead to much more serious consequences than we would care to face (like incarceration or losing a job). Therefore, we choose to hold on to the pain and live our days with the collateral hurt inside of our hearts. We smile like everything is okay while there is a root of bitterness growing from unreleased responses to hurt. In this next phase of forgiveness, you verbalize the frustration, injury, and desired response from the offensive moment. For some, this may be in the form of writing and for others, it may be speaking it aloud. Regardless of which method you choose, the importance is in giving yourself permission to experience your emotions and articulate it. What is verbalized is NOT TO BE CONSIDERED A PLAN OF ACTION BUT AN EXPRESSION OF HURT. In this space, feel free to allow your emotional response to lbe fully expressed and speak the entirety of your heart's pain. An example would be:

"What she did when she gave me an incurable STD made me want to really hurt her physically. It makes me want to end her life because I feel like she ended mine…"

Again I remind you that what is verbalized is NOT TO BE CONSIDERED A PLAN OF ACTION BUT AN EXPRESSION OF EMOTION. As you begin to verbalize it and release it from being trapped in your heart, you will begin to feel various emotions. They will include anger, a possible desire for retaliation, and many other similar emotional responses. You will also begin to gain a sense of the magnitude of the hurt. This is the fullness of the offense becoming present in your heart and mind. You will probably feel the least like forgiving. However, it is at this point where you want to begin the process of forgiveness.

You will need grace for this

Forgiveness, as stated earlier, is not a natural response. It is a God-inspired response. Therefore, it can be futile to attempt to forgive through "natural ability." Therefore, you must begin forgiveness with prayer for grace. Grace is often defined as "unmerited favor" because it opens the door for us to receive spiritual blessings to which we are meritoriously not entitled. However, grace is also a spiritual supplement. It empowers us to receive divine strength in moments of human weakness. Jesus told Paul in 2 Corinthians 12:9, "…My grace is sufficient for you, for power is made perfect in weakness…". Forgiveness is one of those moments when we must rely on the grace of the Lord to give us the ability to do what we cannot and will not do on our own. I would recommend that you pray this simple prayer:

"Lord, give me the grace to release this offense from my heart. I need your strength to help me do this. In Jesus' name I ask it, AMEN."

After praying the prayer, allow a few moments for the Lord to prepare your heart for the process of forgiveness. Once you feel ready to move forward, then go through the next steps.

Pardoning the offense

The first step of forgiveness is to identify and release the person from the "payment" of the offense. Move from being a debt collector to becoming a debt releaser. Name the offense and state verbally:

"I release you from this debt. I choose to no longer hold it against you in such a way that it damages the fellowship between us."

It is important to note that it has to be a matter of the heart as well (Matthew 18:35). Depending on how long this has been in your heart, this may need to happen several times over a series of days and weeks. It takes a lot more effort to remove a tree than a weed from the soil of your heart and mind. As J. Allan Petersen states, "Forgiveness is not an eraser that wipes the memory of the act forever from your mind. That's impossible. It is still history.

The scar may be permanent. To forgive and forget is to forgive the anger we feel toward the person who injured us...Even though we remember the deed, we [eventually] treat the person as though it never happened."[21] Don't be surprised if the issue arises in your heart several more times, just continue to release it until it fully leaves your heart. As R. T. Kendall says, "forgiveness is a lifelong commitment."[22]

Removing the heavenly record

Most models for forgiveness are based upon the premise of God exercising vengeance so that we don't have to. Such an impulse retains the offense but simply uses forgiveness to "wipe their hands clean" while hiring God as a "cosmic hitman" to "take care of the dirty work." Such scriptures as Romans 12:19 are used to validate ungodly retribution. Those scriptures are usually taken out of context when being used for such purposes. In context, they remind us to continue to love and do good to those that hurt us knowing that the offender will have to answer to God for his or her actions. As it pertains to forgiveness, we are to take the position of doing everything in our power to ensure that the person is completely forgiven of the wrongs that they have done. This includes asking the Lord to remove it from His heavenly record. We see Paul exhibits this level of forgiveness in 2 Timothy 4:16b when he says, "…may it not be counted against them." This type of forgiveness I call "dynamic forgiveness" because it seeks to not only clear them socially, but it seeks to clear their "eternal record."

This dynamic forgiveness asks that the Lord remove the offense from heaven's record so that there is no divine punishment for the offense. In order to seek such a level of forgiveness, it requires that the love of God fills our hearts. As Kendall states, "…not to reckon, impute, or 'count' the wrongs of a loved one is to do for that person what God does for us, namely, choose not to recognize their sin."[23] To simply ask for forgiveness can be done out of a social and/or religious mandate for cordial fellowship, but to request pardon at an eternal level requires a selfless, authentic concern for their spiritual well-being. This requires that you put your feelings aside and genuinely desire for them to receive the same grace that you would normally reserve for yourself. This is the same love that Jesus modeled on the cross when He cried out "Father forgive them; for they do not know what they are doing …" (Luke 23:34). Jesus shows us that love is best seen when we are able to release the debt from our hearts while the enemy's "nails and thorns" are still present in our lives.

You may have some sense of reluctance at first. However, as you proceed, I encourage you to ask the Lord to give you the grace to love until you find peace in this person receiving such a level of forgiveness. Use this prayer:

"Father, I ask that you would remove any

offense done by (person's name). Please remove it from your heavenly record and let there be no heavenly retribution for what was done to me."

Pronouncing blessing

The final step in this process of forgiveness is asking the Lord to bless the life of the person that offended you. This is the ultimate manifestation of love. Love seeks to have a person realize the most beneficial outcome even in seasons where they don't merit it. Take a moment to ask the Lord to bless them, their family, ministry work and professional life. The prayer may simply state:

"Father, I now ask that you will bless (person's name). Bless every area of his/her life and bless the work of his/her hands that they may experience your prosperity and favor. Let his/her life not reflect in any way the offense that was done, but allow it to fully reflect Your love towards him/her."

Though this is not the easiest process, it is the primary gateway for healthy fellowship. Every relationship will have a season that includes conflict and forgiveness ensures that the remainder of the post-conflict season doesn't get infected and influenced by the resonating emotional fluctuations that come from withheld and/or unresolved hurt. As author Marianne Williamson stated, "Forgiveness is not always easy. At times, it feels more painful than the wound we suffered, to forgive the one that inflicted it. And yet, there is no peace without forgiveness."

A Look Within...

1. How have you "averted" danger since experiencing your offense? What has it stopped you from doing and with whom has it stopped you from having a relationship?

2. We are often taught to "forgive and forget." Knowing now that forgiveness is not forgetting, how does that change your outlook?

3. Which changes need to take place in your heart so that you will be able to ask God to bless those that hurt you?

The Faith to Reclaim a Healthy Life

> *Forgiveness is believing that the future can be better than the past. The past can't be changed, but God can do something redemptive with it.*

–Adam Hamilton, Forgiveness

In Luke chapter 18, we are introduced to the narrative of a woman that gets healed from an infirmity that has caused her to have a bent over back for 18 years. She is in a crowd of believers, but is clearly suffering with an illness. Jesus notices her and declares to her that she is freed from the spirit that has brought this illness upon her. However, though the spirit has left, her back is still bent over. In essence, Jesus has resolved the spiritual cause but the woman still experiences the collateral damage of its existence.

Many people are like this woman when it

comes to forgiveness. We approach and are healed by Jesus of the emotional existence of the sting and "spiritual bondage" of the offense; but we still house the symptoms that we displayed when it was in our hearts. We forgive others, but still wrestle with depression, fear, doubt, low self-esteem, bitterness and the list goes on.

Jesus realized that the woman needed to experience restoration after the healing. Therefore, He laid His hands on her and her back straightened. Many of us experience forgiveness thinking that it is the only spiritual transaction that we need to address in those spaces where we have been hurt. But in order to experience the fullness of forgiveness, it is going to require that we not just seek to remove the offense, but also open our hearts so that the Lord can restore, recalibrate and reset our healthy life function.

This is where faith is required. When we are deeply hurt or scarred by certain events, they can be so life-shattering that it seems unlikely that life can be restored to the state that existed before it happened. Faith allows us to have the confidence in God's promised outcome, even when we have a difficult time seeing how it will come to pass. Loving after being abused or taking another chance on someone that has previously "burned you" can be hard to imagine (especially when the wound has taken a significant period of time to heal). However, we must learn how to rest in the confidence that God can mend and recover that which had been broken.

As Dr. Sidney Simon points out, forgiveness grants you the opportunity to become a "believer in life" again. He states, "Once you have traveled far enough down that long, winding, often painful road we call the healing process, you will indeed find forgiveness and inner peace waiting for you. Your present will be more powerful than your past, and as a result you will not want to be held back or bogged down by old injuries and injustices. You will let go of them instead."[24]

Though it may not feel like it, on the other side of the hurt, a healthy life awaits. For those that have the courage to attempt to reclaim it, forgiveness can become the gateway to several realities:

1) The ministry of reconciliation (2 Cor. 5:18-20)

Paul reminds us that our salvation and forgiveness of sins was not just for the purpose of clearing an eternal record. The ultimate goal was to facilitate the full reconciliation of our relationship with God. Not only that, but we have been given the same ministry. It's not just about "dropping the charges," forgiveness provides a platform on which reconciliation can take place. Reconciliation suggests that the relationship looks like the offense has been fully resolved and harmony has been restored.

Forgiveness opens the door to laugh again, work together and co-exist in a space characterized by collaboration and cordiality.

2) The restoration of fellowship (Matt. 18:15)

When we are able to forgive, we "gain a brother." Anyone that has ever been hurt knows the disconnect that offenses bring into our lives and relationships. When we have been offended, it causes a breach in fellowship that creates a wedge between those involved. We begin to re-examine and redefine relationships based upon how much we have been hurt and how "loving" and close we "feel" they are to us. This response causes family members to not speak for years, co-workers to feel distant though they are sitting next to each other, and church members to leave ministries (and possibly even congregations).

When we forgive from our hearts and have

the courage to reconcile, the walls that we build and the chasms that we forge between one another are removed and the breach is restored. Our lives become, once again, enriched by the presence of those that were intended to be there. The brotherhood or sisterhood that we once knew is resurrected and we are able to be nourished by the camaraderie and fellowship that they bring.

3) A reflection of God's love (Matt. 5:45)

There are few experiences in our walks in Christ that allow us to sense the immensity of the love of God as forgiveness does. When we are able to allow our faith to guide us to forgive, we learn the love of God at an entirely different level. After forgiveness and restoration, we come to discover the power of the Spirit of God within us to produce a supernatural love through us. We then exist at a level that is more apt to take risks and let go of interpersonal disputes, because we operate in the newfound understanding that nothing that hurts us can fully diminish the possibility of love that rests in us. Therefore, we embrace a new height of unconditional love towards all without fear of failure.

4) A new perspective of others (Col. 1:21-22)

On the other side of forgiveness, our view of others gets reset. We begin to rediscover the other side of the person's character that our hurt prevented us from seeing. The new openness to their "true" personality reminds us that that they are truly more of a blessing to our lives than a burden. As Adam Hamilton states, "…what would happen if you erased the debit column altogether, if you decided that, when it comes to the small stuff, you're only going to remember the positives?...Choose to keep track of the blessings your partner brings into your life. A ledger that is weighted toward the positive is a big help in letting a relationship soar…First Corinthians 13, [Paul] writes, 'Love keeps no record of wrongs.' When we change our accounting procedure, we begin to find more joy in our relationships."[25]

Setting boundaries after forgiveness

There are some offenses that are of such a detrimental nature that the level of reconciliation may need to be considered. In cases where a person has a mental illness, an unhealthy habit that places others in harm's way, or a spiritual issue that remains unresolved, it is necessary that we exercise precaution with what we entrust to that person's care. The presence of forgiveness does not mean the absence of wisdom. In cases where the possibility of repeated harm is likely, we must reconcile with the person, but be careful of how we position our possessions. It may not be wise to leave your child with a person that has a habitual pattern of child abuse or have a person with a gambling sickness hold your cash for an extended period of time. As Solomon stated, "Wisdom is the principal thing."

Forgiveness deals with past sins and must be accompanied by mountains of mercy. Reconciliation deals with present fellowship and must be accompanied by love and wisdom. Whether or not we reconcile is not the question. Whether or not we reconcile using wisdom is.

From your hurt comes their hope

In Luke 23, Jesus reminds Peter that Satan would sift him as wheat. However, He encourages Peter, "after you have turned back, strengthen your brethren." Because the offense happens to us, it is not uncommon that we assume that the entire experience is about us. Though we go through and grow from what happens to us, we are not the ultimate audience that the Lord has in mind. The suffering that happens in our lives and bodies has been divinely orchestrated to translate into strength and optimism in the lives of others. Our story gives us the platform to speak encouragement and hope into the lives of others that are either navigating the waters of the storm or resting on the shores in the calm before the storm.

Refuse to leave the dusk of hurt and not allow yourself to be guided into the dawn of a renewed life. The next chapter of a healthy life awaits you if you harness the faith embrace it.

A Prayer to Reclaim a Healthy Life

Heavenly Father, thank you for giving me the grace to forgive. Now I ask that you give me the faith and courage to know that the health of the fellowship that was lost can be restored. Guard my heart against any spiritual attacks that will encourage me to not move into the fullness of life that you have ordained for me. Help me to rest in the divine assurance that hope is just as real as the hurt that has impacted my life. Thank you for the new life that you are birthing in my heart, mind and relationships. Grant me the grace to move forward with love and wisdom. In Jesus' name, I ask this. AMEN

A Look Within...

1. Imagine life after forgiveness of the offense. What does this look like? What is different? How have things improved?

2. If you've ever forgiven an offense, how did your perspective of the offender change for the better?

3. With a difficult offense/offender in mind, what are some boundaries that you can develop and implement?

4. How can you use your offenses and journey to/through forgiveness to help another person that is wrestling with forgiving?

A Closing Word...

This book was never about you. It pointed to your story and walked you through your emotional process, but it wasn't about you. It was about making sure that you walk away with a testimony that could give someone else faith during his or her testing moments. Your survival will determine someone else's outcome. You must forgive so that they can give themselves permission to live. Go forth to make an eternal imprint on the hearts of those that you will encourage as you exhibit the faith to forgive.

-James McCarroll

Endnotes

Chapter 1

1	Hogue, Rodney. Forgiveness (Abilene: Rodney Hogue, 2008) 61.

2	Bevere, John. The Bait of Satan (Lake Mary: Charisma House, 2004) 121.

3	This is a quote from the "Peace Prayer" attributed Saint Francis.

Chapter 2

4	De La Forét, Rosalee. Alchemy of Herbs (Carlsbad: Hay House, 2017), 119.

Chapter 3

5	Brown, Brené. Daring Greatly (New York: Penguin Random House, 2012), 67.

6	Demoss, Nancy. Choosing Forgiveness. (Chicago: Moody Publishers, 2006) 79.

7   Demoss, 80.
8   Hanh, Thich Naht. Fear: Essential Wisdom for Getting through the Storm (New York: HarperOne, 2006) 17.
9   Patricia Resick, Candice Monson, and Kathleen Chard. Cognitive Processing Theory for PTSD: A Comprehensive Manual (New York: The Guilford Press, 2017)
10   Hogue, 48.
11   Kelly, Matthew. Resisting Happiness (North Palm Beach: Beacon Publishing, 2016) 110.

12   Simon, Dr. Sidney and Suzanne. Forgiveness: How to Make Peace with Your Past and Get on with Your Life (New York: Warner Books, 1990) 46.

13   Demoss, 59.
14   Simon, 124-125.

Chapter 4

15   Lieberman, Matthew. Social: Why Our Brains are Wired to Connect (New York: Broadway Books, 2013) 212.

16   Haidt, Jonathan. The Happiness Hypothesis: Finding Modern Truth in Ancient Wisdom (New York: Basic Books, 2006) 146.

17   Hogue, 12.
18   Simon, 15-18
19   Simon, 18-19
20   Hogue, 27.
21   Peterson, J. Allan. The Myth of Greener Grass (Wheaton: Tyndale House, 1989) 145.
22   Kendall, 185
23   Ibid., 137-138

Chapter 5

24   Simon, 206.

25   Hamilton, 45